MW01031341

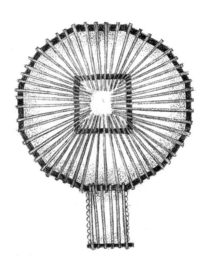

Copyright © 2009 by Jonathan Horning

Published by
Walker Publishing Company, Inc., New York

Printed on recycled paper.

Library of Congress Cataloging-in-Publication Data
has been applied for.

ISBN 978-0-8027-1773-3

Visit Walker & Company's Web site
at www.walkerbooks.com

First U.S. edition 2009

1 3 5 7 9 10 8 6 4 2

Designed and typeset by
Wooden Books Ltd, Glastonbury, UK

Printed in the United States of America

SIMPLE SHELTERS

TENTS, TIPIS, YURTS, DOMES AND OTHER ANCIENT HOMES

written and illustrated by

Jonathan Horning

with additional material by Brock Horning

Walker & Company, New York

To Amanda,

with love, chocolate, and roses

Thank you

Thanks to the other team members: Brock for his truly outstanding contribution to the text, and John, firstly for his expertise and wizardry on every aspect of book publication, and secondly, along with Suzi and Aggie for their fantastic hospitality throughout. Thanks to Charlie Dancey and René Müller for help with domes.

I have drawn from many sources in researching this book. The following texts were invaluable: Native American Architecture *by P Nabokov & R. Easton,* Shelter *edited by Lloyd Kahn,* Dwellings *and* Shelter in Africa *by P. Oliver,* Tents *by T. Faegre,* Bamboo *by O. Hidalgo-Lopez,* Bamboo *by K Dunkelberg,* Order In Space *by Keith Critchlow,* The Gothic Vault *by J. Acland,* African Traditional Architecture *by Susan Denyer,* and Bender Heaven *by Laugh. Visit simplydifferently.org for information on domes.*

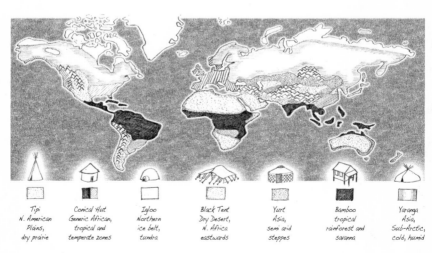

A map of the world, showing climate zones and the types of shelters found in them.

CONTENTS

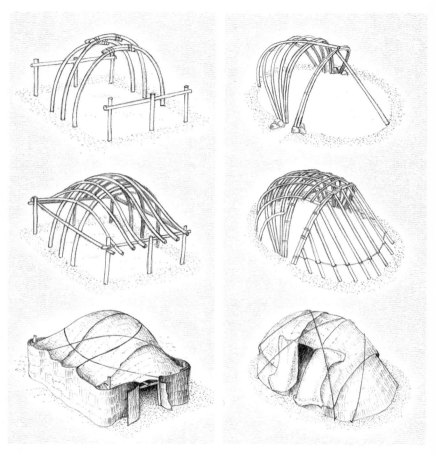

Two unusual African nomadic shelters using bent and straight wood.
Left: Shelter of the Tuareg tribe, S Sahara, made from the acacia tree and covered in palm matting.
Right: Shelter of the Rendille tribe, Kenya, constructed of available sticks and wild sisal knotted
fibre mats, along with cow hides.

INTRODUCTION

Despite their simple form, shelters are far from simplistic. A detailed knowledge of nature, and some finely honed skills are required to modify the environment successfully in such a way as to survive the harsh conditions that occur around the world. All the ancient shelters featured in this little book evolved as functional responses to local climate, the availability of materials, and temporal requirements, nomadic, seasonal or settled. Some are designed to be carried around, others stand for years. Almost all fade back into the landscape with little or no damage nor waste.

Traditional shelters not only provide an excellent snapshot of the many ingenious ways in which mankind has perfected the art of protection, they also clearly demonstrate how their inhabitants operate as a conscious part of nature. In addition, many if not all ancient dwellings symbolise the entirety of creation for the tribes and peoples who live in them, providing a constant reminder of their place within the universe, a summary of their traditions and perception of wholeness. This is perhaps most simply reflected in the almost exclusive circular plan of early human shelters, which also represent the circle of the year, and the cyclical patterns of nomadic existence.

More recent techniques of straw bale construction and geodesic domes are included because of their ingenuity and building simplicity. The definition of a simple shelter is obviously personal, but I hope that you, the reader, will try to build at least one of the lovely homes in these pages at some point in your life, and spend a dream filled night in it.

PRIMARY FORMS
elementary structures

Shelters are almost as old as Adam. Their primary and oldest function is the provision of protection, whether against rain, sleet, snow, freezing fog, sunshine, wind and extreme temperatures, or foes such as insects, wolves, big cats or enemies. A secondary, and possibly more recent, function is their provision of comfort, and visual and auditory privacy.

The very earliest shelters used by mankind were natural features, trees, hollows, caves or rock overhangs. The earliest known huts are conical Ukrainian structures, dated to 14,000 BC, built of pine poles and mammoth bones. Most early shelters across the world are based on the circle or triangle, the strongest and most structurally sound shapes.

Huts with circular bases suit materials with low load-bearing strength as they distribute weight equally between all frame members. Shelters using the triangle often take the form of triangular prisms, which are better braced against gravity but provide little height. The two shapes merge in the conical tent, and all can be covered with anything at hand; earth, animal skins, leaves, or sticks.

Shown opposite are the primary forms which occur universally across the world, elements of which we will meet throughout these pages.

bone and skin shelter

nomadic Anglo-Saxon A-frame

elementary forms derived by lashing one, two, and three poles together

Aboriginal bark A-Frame

woodland log lean to

conical variations

utilising fewer long poles

inclusion of a smoke ring

development of elementary forms on to a circular plan

Tupiq, Inuit summer dwellings

development on to rectangular and semi circular plans

'half benders' singles or couplets

3

TENSIONED COVERINGS
taut to stand

Although most shelters rely primarily on covered frames, where the frame provides the wall strength, many early and temporary shelters rely significantly on tension for their structure. Some large dwellings, such as nomadic black tents (*shown overleaf*), also have little frame structure and rely significantly on the tension of the covering. Indeed, most tents today rely on tension to a large extent for their stability.

Tensioned coverings require fabrics or skins which can be pulled taut, and the main tensioned claddings available to ancient peoples were animal hides and woven sheets of spun animal hair or hemp fibre. Sewn together, coverings made of these materials can stretch without splitting or breaking. Most other coverings such as earth, matting, or felt can only be used on self-supporting structures.

All tensioned structures need a vertical support, whether a small internal frame secured by ropes, or an external support such as a tree. They can then be pegged or weighted down with rocks to define the space, either directly on to the ground to create walls and fully enclose the interior or, in hot areas, by fastening to the ground via ropes so that the inhabitants can catch any through-wind and remain cool.

ridge pole with tensioned cover

variation with longitudinal support

4

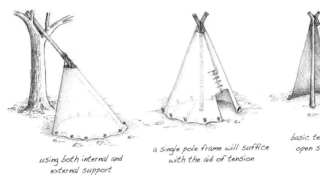

using both internal and
external support

a single pole frame will suffice
with the aid of tension

basic tensioned
open shelter

no internal frame means that external
support is needed

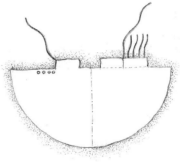

contemporary canvas tent plan for the
examples shown above and left

just ropes and
external support

a square of tensioned cover makes an
effective shelter, as in black tents

BLACK TENTS
houses of hair

The best way to understand general principles is to study examples. There are two main types of black tent, the more simple Eastern or Persian type, found from Iran to Tibet and the Western type, used from north west Africa to Arabia, Iraq, and Syria. In the Eastern type the cloth breadths are sewn together lengthways in one direction with the tension running along the seams (otherwise they would rend). The poles are placed under the seams with loops at the edges for the rope stays. The Western type uses the same basic principle, but has tension bands running across the cloth breadths so that the main pull is concentrated across these seams, which are supported by the poles and rope stays and attached to stay fasteners at either end.

Limited resources mean that the use of wood is minimal, something which is only possible in a tensile structure. The entire tension of the cover is collected in a few key points, meaning that the cover and frame are interdependent, neither can stand without the other.

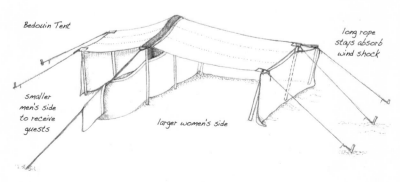

Bedouin Tent

long rope stays absorb wind shock

smaller men's side to receive guests

larger women's side

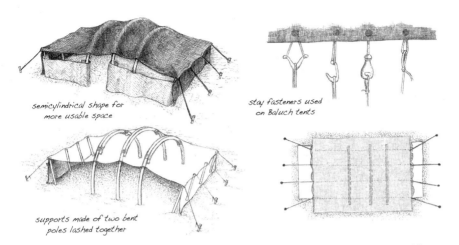

semicylindrical shape for more usable space

stay fasteners used on Baluch tents

supports made of two bent poles lashed together

Upper page: The Eastern-type barrel-vaulted black tent of the Baluchi from Afghanistan has adapted the ancient arched hut in its design. Less tension is needed because of the wooden supports.

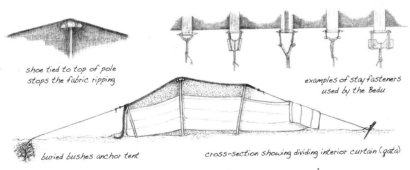

shoe tied to top of pole stops the fabric ripping

examples of stay fasteners used by the Bedu

buried bushes anchor tent

cross-section showing dividing interior curtain (qata)

Lower page: Bedouin black tent with Western-style tension bands. To the roof rectangle are pinned two exterior curtains (ruaq) which enclose the sides and at least one interior decorated curtain (qata) to divide the sexes. These can be removed to catch any through wind. The well-decorated end of the interior curtain is hung out over the rope stay to signify the entrance.

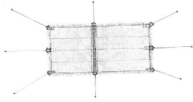

7

MORE BLACK TENTS
full of western promise

Black tent territory spreads from the north-west coast of Africa to the eastern border of Tibet. Primarily developed and created for hot and dry desert conditions, the roof is low to shield from the sun and sandstorms but open to catch cooling through-winds. The covering is made primarily from dark goat hair, from which the name is derived, chosen for its strength, length, and tensile qualities. Sometimes camel hair and sheep's wool are also mixed in. Its dark hue ensures dense shade and helps heat escape in hot weather, but also makes it a good insulator in cold weather. Its open weave allows hot air to pass out while the hair's natural oils create an effective shield against all but the heaviest rains.

At the end of a typical five to six year life span, these tents will completely decompose back into the environment. Those shown here are among many used by the different tribes, and all differ slightly according to climatic differences, tribal identity and customs.

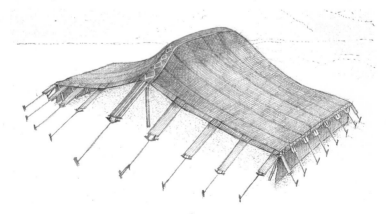

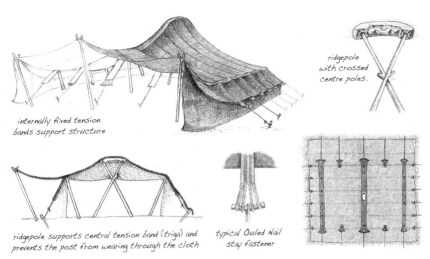

internally fixed tension
bands support structure

ridgepole
with crossed
centre poles.

ridgepole supports central tension band (triga) and
prevents the post from wearing through the cloth

typical Ouled Nail
stay fastener

Upper page: Western-type tent of the Ouled Nail from Algeria. Cloth breadths made 2-3 feet wide and 30-60
feet long and colored according to tribal colors for identification.

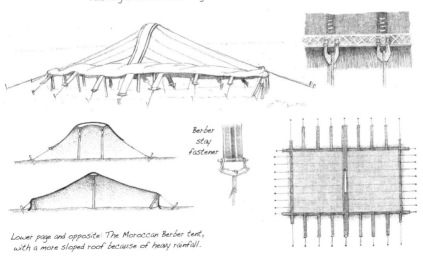

Berber
stay
fastener

Lower page and opposite: The Moroccan Berber tent,
with a more sloped roof because of heavy rainfall.

9

SIMPLE BENDERS
temporary temples

Benders can be found in different styles across America, Africa, Asia and Lapland. They are universal dwellings, suitable for many different climates and terrains, and they are also one of the easiest shelters to create, requiring no complex tools, merely thin wood saplings. Cut green poles are bent (hence the name) to form a hemisphere, and this framework is covered with whatever is locally available. Native North Americans use elm and birch bark for their wigwam, Finnish Laps use caribou skins, and some tribes in Africa create reed mats, which allow hot air to escape and so keep the interior cool. Benders, however, are limited in size and can only support a limited amount of weight.

There are three main ways to begin building a bender. The first involves sticking both ends of a pole into the ground, arching it overhead. The second uses poles with one end stuck into the ground, bent towards each other, overlapped and tied together overhead, while the third method collects the pole ends together into a central point.

As in all traditional shelters local choice and availability affects what wood is used but willow is a common choice. Others widely used are elm, hazel, hickory, basswood and hemlock.

Congolese leaf cladding

Lappish skin cladding

Fulani reed mat cladding

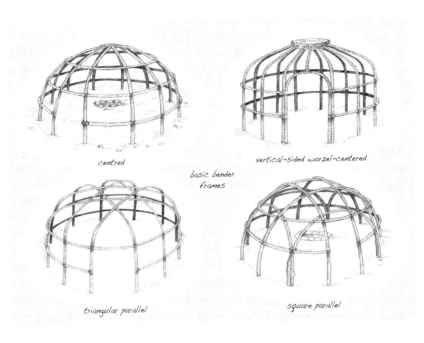

centred

vertical-sided worzel-centered

basic bender frames

triangular parallel

square parallel

Native North American wigwam showing simultaneous interior and exterior frame to keep elm and birch bark cladding in place. Bark is peeled from trees with a wedge or axe after cutting a serrated ring. Strips are sewn together with spruce root.

BIGGER BENDERS
with internal support structures

Larger and more complex benders need internal support. For example, wigwams (*below*) were developed in woodlands and have a sapling frame lashed together at a point to create an approx 20ft diameter arch, 9–10ft high. The frame is supported by two interior posts connected by a crossbeam. Horizontal stringers are tied around the frame in tiers to strengthen it and support the covering of woven reed or grass mats or birch, elm, or chestnut tree bark in sheets 8–10ft long and 4ft wide.

The Ki (*opposite top*), from subtropical woodlands, uses an 8ft square internal structure of four cottonwood posts joined by crossbeams. Sticks placed on top of these create the roof. Willow ribs pushed into the ground are bent onto the crossbeams giving a 15–20ft diameter and 8–9ft high shelter. Local brush and stalks are woven into the frame, before the roof is sealed with mud, and earth is banked against the walls.

The Wichita grasshouse (*lower opposite*) has a frame of poles bent over an interior 10ft diameter ring of 8 or 12 posts and connecting beams. All but the first four cardinal poles (which extend to the apex) are tied into a ring at the top leaving a smoke hole. Stringers strengthen the frame and grass is tied on in tight bunches with exterior stringers holding it in place.

Kickapoo tribe
Wigwam

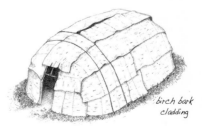

birch bark
cladding

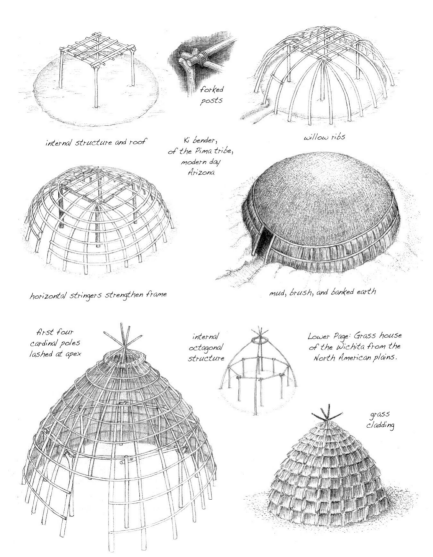

internal structure and roof

forked posts

Ki bender, of the Pima tribe, modern day Arizona

willow ribs

horizontal stringers strengthen frame

mud, brush, and banked earth

first four cardinal poles lashed at apex

internal octagonal structure

Lower Page: Grass house of the Wichita from the North American plains.

grass cladding

WOVEN AND CONICAL
inverted baskets

An unusual variation of bent wood structures are the woven examples shown here, home to sedentary farmers from southern Ethiopia, and suiting hot, humid, and occasionally rainy conditions.

The oval Chencha house of the Dorze tribe begins as a 24 ft circle drawn with a bamboo and string compass. Split bamboo poles are then placed 4 inches apart, and horizontal bands woven around this frame, working upwards. Near the top, the frame members are bent inwards and almost closed at the 24 ft peak. A tapering woven porch is added with a wooden or bamboo woven door, barred from inside. Tight layers of waterproof bamboo leaf and straw thatch are placed onto the frame, slid under bamboo strips, again working upwards. Inside, the space is divided into two by a bamboo partition. The back is used for storage; the front is home to a central fire, smoke venting through openings halfway up.

The Tukul house of the Sidama people uses a central support pole and a waterproof savannah grass or bamboo thatch placed between two layers of wickerwork. The interior is divided between human and cattle, a woven bamboo screen also dividing the parental room from the living area where children and guests sleep. Here there is also a hearth in the centre.

The 10–16 ft hut of the Gurage tribe begins with a slight circular ditch with split eucalyptus stuck vertically into the ground and tied in a circle with halved bamboo rope. Rafters are fixed to a central pole leaving a 3 ft protrusion at the top and tied with parallel circles of rope running around the building, supported by beams. The roof is thatched from bottom to top with dried grass and the inside wall is covered with two layers of mud. This building lasts 30–50 years but needs a thatch replacement every ten.

Chencha house framework and covering.
When the frame member bottoms rot, the house
is cut from its base and replanted, lowering the
house 8" every 4 years, until too low to use,
when a new one is built.

Sidamo house framework and covering.
5.5ft vertical poles are grounded in a 20-24ft
circle. Split bamboo are woven in between for the
walls. The roof is made separately, put into place,
and supported by the central pole (far right).

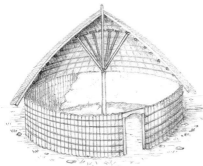

Gurage house. A common African form with
a conical roof mounted on a cylindrical base.
Here, diagonal beams supporting the rafters
are projected 10ft up the central pole. Larger
houses have another set 5ft higher.

15

TIPIS

the smartest of conical tents

The Native American tipi evolved in the temperate climate of the North American Plains. Easy to put up and take down, it was used to follow the great herds of buffalo. Early tipis were transported by dogs and were small, averaging 12 ft across with 15 ft poles. At this time, many Native American nations were semi–nomadic, living in tipis in summer and earth lodges in winter (*see page 28*). Later, with horses, tipis became larger, 18–20 ft diameter with 21–25 ft poles. Being able to cover more distance in a day, tribes followed the herds all year round, becoming totally nomadic. The cover was folded and packed on a travois and the poles bundled together and dragged along.

Lodgepole pine grew plentifully on the plains and was the preferred wood for the poles. Good sets of lodgepoles were very valuable. The cover was made from around 12 tanned buffalo hides, a number of curing processes keeping them soft, flexible and water-resistant. A new tipi would also have smudge fires lit inside to ensure water-resistancy. Covers were usually replaced every 1–3 years but could last up to a decade if necessary. Painted or decorated covers were reserved for the tipis of specially-honoured people or medicine men. The design was often based on a visionary dream, encouraged by sacred rites.

A tipi can be erected within an hour. First a foundation of either 3 or 4 poles is tied together, the rope hanging down to the ground to anchor the tent. Upon this are placed 20–30 lighter poles (four-pole foundations generally have more of these lighter poles than those with three). Then the cover is tied to a lifting pole, usually the longest, wrapped into place and fixed together with wooden pins.

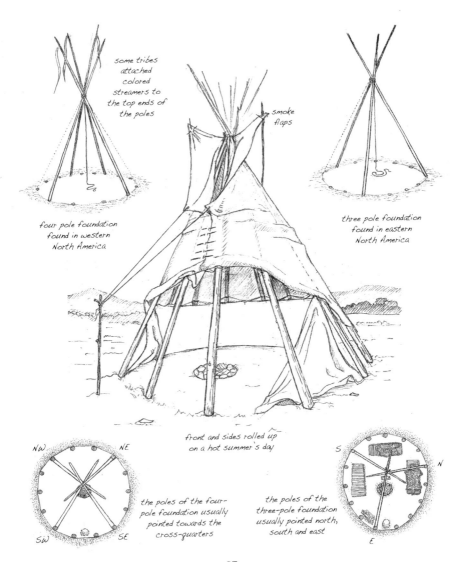

some tribes attached colored streamers to the top ends of the poles

smoke flaps

four pole foundation found in western North America

three pole foundation found in eastern North America

front and sides rolled up on a hot summer's day

NW   NE

SW   SE

the poles of the four-pole foundation usually pointed towards the cross-quarters

S   N

E

the poles of the three-pole foundation usually pointed north, south and east

17

MORE TIPIS
of the North American Plains

Inside a traditional tipi, a geometrically decorated 'dew cloth', or inner lining, hangs to the floor to insulate and prevent draughts caused by the wind or air drawn in for the fire. It also keeps rain running down the poles away from the living area, and during extreme cold creates a pocket which can be stuffed with grass for extra insulation. Early tipis tended to be weighted down with rocks, pegs later taking their place.

Traditionally, tipis are pitched by women, on small hillocks so the floor stays dry, and facing east to welcome the morning sun and protect against the prevailing west wind. Inside, men sit to the north, women to the south, and any honored guests to the west. In the centre, an altar stands on which fragrant herbs are burned, carrying prayers to the Great Spirit, with a hearth just to the east of it. Sacred medicine bundles hang on tripods inside the tipi, while firewood, food and cooking implements are kept near the door.

Tipis differ from other conical tents in two main ways: the backward tilt, which helps brace against the wind and increases usable interior space, and the use of a smoke flap, which channels wind, drawing the smoke out. The smoke flap can be adjusted to the wind direction or closed completely in rain or snow.

Tipi door flaps take many forms; three styles are shown below.

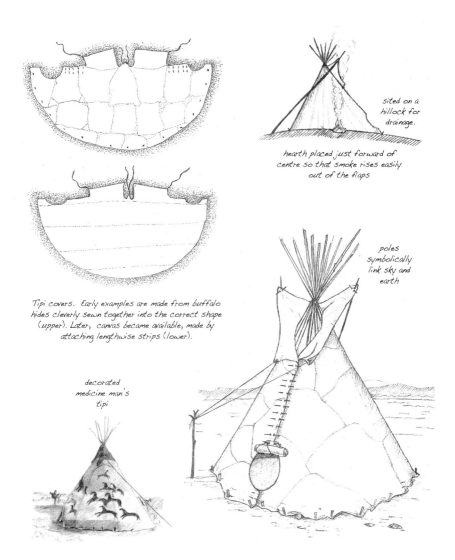

sited on a hillock for drainage.

hearth placed just forward of centre so that smoke rises easily out of the flaps

poles symbolically link sky and earth

Tipi covers. Early examples are made from buffalo hides cleverly sewn together into the correct shape (upper). Later, canvas became available, made by attaching lengthwise strips (lower).

decorated medicine man's tipi

19

KATHE
strong curves

There are three types of Lapland kathe: forked-pole, curved-pole, and turf. The forked-pole kathe (*not shown*) is a cone of forked poles beginning with a three pole foundation upon which 20–30 poles are added and is the summer home of the forest Lapps.

The curved-pole kathe (*opposite top*) is a unique lightweight structure which uses a curved rafter frame to give a large diameter space. Two pairs of curved pole rafters are cut from naturally bow-shaped pines or birches and threaded onto an overhead smoke pole with cross-pieces halfway down. Two bent door posts are threaded onto the front and a single pole onto the back (*see below*). Against this strong framework are tied 12–18 slender poles 9–15ft long. Inside, the hearth is in the centre, a ring of flat stones, with the kitchen area opposite the door and storage near the door, the rest of the space forms the living and sleeping areas.

The turf kathe (*lower opposite*) is used as a permanent home for coastal Lapps and a winter home for the semi-nomadic forest Lapps. It employs the same basic frame as the curved-pole kathe but is heavier and covered with earth and logs.

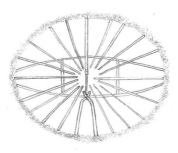

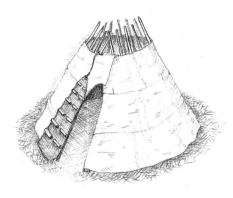

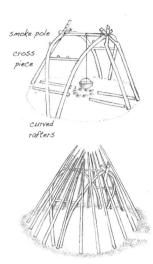

smoke pole

cross
piece

curved
rafters

The curved-pole kathe. The cover is in two halves fixed at
the back pole and tied to the front door posts. The door
is made of skins or cloth and attached to wooden battens
to hold it against the posts. Anchor stones placed inside
the tent hold down the bottom edge of the cover.

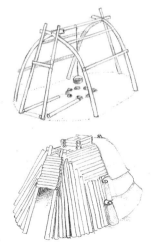

The turf kathe is similar to the curved pole kathe in that
it uses two curved poles at either end connected by the
'smoke pole' and middle cross beams. This kathe, being a
permanent dwelling, is generally made of heavier, thicker poles
and covered with logs and bark before being buried in earth.

21

YURTS
freestanding felt

Yurt territory stretches from eastern Turkey to Mongolia with concentrations in Mongolia, Kazakhstan and Kyrgyzstan (where many people still live in them today). Freestanding structures, normally 10–20 ft in diameter, yurts rely on opposing pressures for rigidity: the downward and outward forces from the weight of the roof are balanced by the inward compression of a tension band around the top of the walls, meaning that it holds its shape without the need for guy lines or a stretched cover.

There are four essential parts to a yurt: the walls (*khana*), roof poles (*uni*), crown (*tono, two regional examples shown below*) and door frame (*nars*). The collapsible trellis walls are made of 6–8 sections of trellis, each containing around twenty 6–7 ft poles and four half poles held together with knotted leather thongs. The door frame is lashed to the trellis with horsehair rope. Overhead, steam-bent roundwood poles use a string loop at one end to attach to the wall and are tapered at the other to fit into the crown socket. The crown itself is a circular wheel, 3–6 ft in diameter with spokes to raise the centre and support the crown cover.

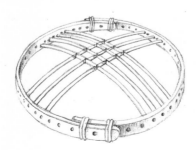
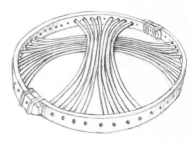

The Bentwood yurt is found from eastern Turkey to northern China. Steam-bent roof poles raise the interior height and support a light crown of two bent semi-circular split saplings lashed together with rawhide. The yurt uses unsplit willow, whose natural taper gives maximum strength for minimum weight. The wood is often slightly charred to repel insects. In construction, three poles are inserted into the crown and tied onto the trellis wall, before the rest are added.

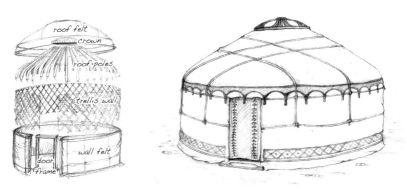

roof felt
crown
roof poles
trellis wall
wall felt
door frame

Above left: the different sections of a yurt. Above right: Bentwood yurt with felt covering and curtain door. Some areas use reed mats in summer to let air circulate and add felt underneath in winter for insulation.

23

MORE YURTS
homes for all seasons

Yurt covers are traditionally made of felt, created by beating and rolling wet sheep's fleece. Three overlapping layers of felt are normally used, although in winter up to five extra layers can be added. A crown cover smoke flap is tied into place from within, which can be moved to suit the wind or cover the top completely in the event of rain. Felt insulates well, and its natural oils give some water resistance, but it has little or no tensile strength and so can only be used on self-supporting structures. While the frame can last a lifetime, the felt has to be replaced every 10–20 years, the worn out covers being used for insulation under rugs on the floor.

Yurts are incredibly versatile. In the winter, earth is banked against the sides, and the floor covered with a layer of grass and worn out felt, while in the summer, the door and sides can be rolled up, drawing cool air in and pushing hot air out of the crown. When travelling, the crown, a few roof poles, and some felt can be used as a very temporary shelter, while an expanded trellis wall can also be used as a sheep fold. As with most nomadic tents, a yurt can be taken down by experienced travellers and be made ready for transit in under an hour.

The nomadic Shah Savan of the Azerbaijan Province of Iran use a yurt-like structure called an Alachigh (*lower opposite*).

  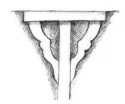

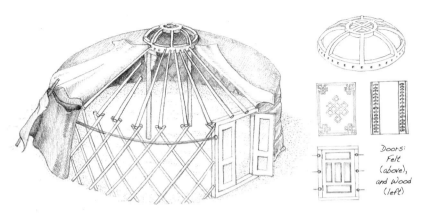

Doors:
Felt
(above),
and Wood
(left)

The Mongolian 'ger'. The heavy crown rests on two decorated roof posts (bagana – shown lower opposite). During construction the crown is lashed to the posts and held in place while the roof poles, which are traditionally straight, are inserted and tied to the trellis wall. The crown is made of mortice and tenoned wood with eight or ten spokes.

Alachigh six-fold domed crown; a smoke cover is placed over it similar to a yurt.

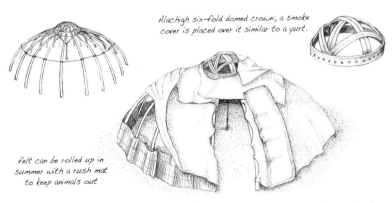

felt can be rolled up in summer with a rush mat to keep animals out

The Alachigh of the Shah Savan from Iran covers as large an area as a yurt with less wood and so is easier to transport. To erect, one man holds the crown while others place between 24 and 32 curved poles into the crown and then into the ground. Woven bands loop around the poles to strengthen the frame and a rope is tied around the crown and staked to the ground. The frame is covered with three felt sheets pegged and tied down.

YARANGA AND CHORAMA DYU
sturdy Siberian structures

Yarangas are shelters used by the Koryak and Chukchi tribes of Siberia, nomadic reindeer farmers, to survive the cold, wet and windy climate. These unique structures remain standing in some of the most intense snows and winds in the world.

An initial tripod of 10–16 ft poles is placed in the ground, around which are placed 4–5 ft long stakes in a 30 ft circle of tripods or pairs. Horizontal poles are tied onto these to form a ring, and roof poles lashed on, which meet overhead. T-poles with curved top pieces are positioned under the roof poles to push them outwards so that snow blows over and does not collect on the roof. Covers are made of around 40 reindeer skins in several pieces, with walrus gut sections sometimes inserted to let in light, and are bound to the frame with ropes which are then pegged to the ground, the lower ends having first been tucked in and weighed down with stones. In summer, the cover is changed for reindeer suede or worn out winter coverings, while in especially cold weather snow is heaped about the walls for insulation. Inside, the perimeter is divided into three to eight *pologs* or interior skin tents to segregate families and create some privacy.

A similar, but smaller and lighter, shelter is the 10 ft chorama dyu used by the Evenk and Yukaghir tribes, also from Siberia. This has at its heart a pyramid of four poplar or willow poles. The cover is in five sections, three for the roof and two for the walls, made of dressed, dehaired reindeer skins, dehairing making them lighter but not as warm. In summer the skins are replaced by a double layer of birch bark, both types of covering being held down by wind rods.

The yaranga, showing internal tripod structure. Several families live inside, each with their own area around the perimeter while sharing the central fire. A Chukchi tent is smaller, housing 3-4 families, whereas a Koryak tent is bigger, housing 6-8.

Yaranga frame in construction

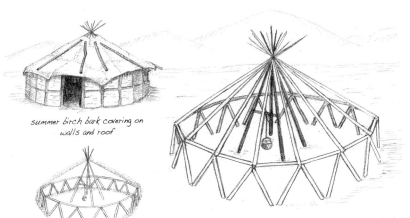

summer birch bark covering on walls and roof

Chorama dyu frame in construction

The small 10ft diameter chorama dyu, showing the internal four-pole pyramid structure. A horizontal pole is tied between these to hang cooking pots over the fire.

EARTH LODGES & PIT HOUSES
in the belly of the earth

Earth lodges (*opposite*) were once built across the globe from England to Finland, Siberia, Japan, and the North American plains. They typically last for around ten years. Construction starts with a central square of posts surrounded by a 40–60 ft diameter circle of shorter poles and beams which extend the space. Rafters resting between them support a lattice of willow covered with an insulating layer of sod and earth. Some North American tribes finish with a layer of wet earth. In Lapland, the entrance is a tunnel, with buffalo skin doors at either end.

Pit houses (*below*) are found in colder climates such as Siberia. Dug 3–4 ft into the earth, sometimes lower, the roof rafters are also buried 2 ft. The sunken level provides height and insulation. Typically 25–40 ft across, they use four main posts to support four primary roof poles. Rafters spaced in concentric circles on the roof leave an opening which doubles as entrance and smoke hole, with a ladder placed into the entrance, resting on the eastern edge of the opening. Walls made of poles support the mud and turf outside, while earth dug from the pit is piled on top. In its first spring grass grows over the pit house, blending it into the environment. Sometimes six central posts and beams are used instead of four, and the house is occasionally rectangular instead of circular.

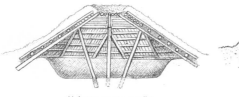

pit house cross-section

four post pit house

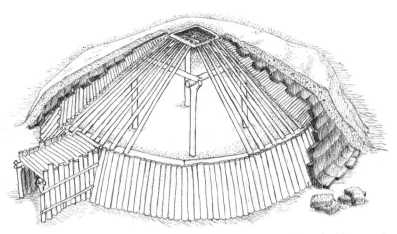

Above: An earth lodge. A lattice of willow covers the frame and supports a layer of prairie grass and a final coat of earth and sod. Like all Native American shelters the entrance faces east.

oak was preferred for the frame but cottonwood was more available

pit house showing lowered floor and buried roof posts with earth lodge frame

earth lodge 'crown'

earth lodge cross-section, showing long entrance passage

grass grows on the earth-covered roof, blending it back into the landscape

LOG CABINS
deep in the woods

Log cabins first evolved in heavily wooded areas such as Scandinavia, Eastern Europe, and Russia, only later appearing in America with European immigration. They employ the weight of timber rather than its tensile qualities and so consume a lot of wood relative to the shelter size to produce strong buildings, well-insulated against frost and foe.

Placed directly on the earth, early buildings consist of logs, with or without bark, stacked on top of each other in opposite directions to account for natural taper, the resultant gap being stuffed with wet earth. Later buildings are raised onto a low stone sill to prevent moisture and rot. They used cleverly notched corner joints and lengthwise shaping to minimise the gap, assist water run off, and prevent wall slippage. Roofs are generally pitched with a robust ridge and purlins supporting the rafters, on top of which is placed a waterproof layer of bark topped off with an insulating layer of turf.

Early log cabins are usually single-roomed, around 12 by 16 ft, with a single door and some windows covered with animal hide, although some have multiple rooms and even two stories. Floors are mostly of earth, sometimes of laid puncheons. Sleeping and storage lofts are common in taller cabins, reached by pegs in the wall or a tree-limb ladder.

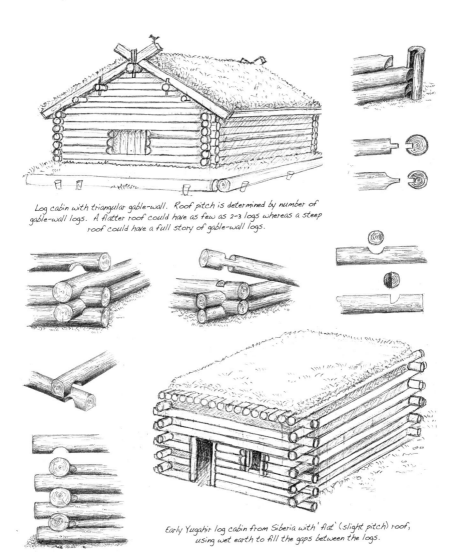

Log cabin with triangular gable-wall. Roof pitch is determined by number of gable-wall logs. A flatter roof could have as few as 2-3 logs whereas a steep roof could have a full story of gable-wall logs.

Early Yugahir log cabin from Siberia with 'flat' (slight pitch) roof, using wet earth to fill the gaps between the logs.

HOGANS
homely places

Hogans are homes of the Navajo tribe and developed in a hot, arid environment. Despite many variations there are three main styles: the iconic early, forked-pole hogan (*opposite top*), of which more in a moment, the 18th century 10–30 ft long four-sided leaning log hogan (*below*), used as a winter dwelling or summer shade, and the 19th century 20 ft diameter corbeled log-roof hogan (*lower opposite*). All are single-roomed structures with a hearth at the centre and an east-facing door.

The origins of the forked-pole ceremonial hogan are steeped in mythology, recounted in songs and chants. Construction begins with a forked south pole and straight north pole, symbolizing gender unity, before a west pole is added to form a tripod. Two door posts to the east complete the main frame. All poles are of juniper wood 10–12 ft long producing a 12–20 ft diameter. Upon this frame thinner poles are leant and covered with six inches of earth. Inside, men sit to the south with their hunting gear and tools, and women to the north with their cooking implements and looms. Opposite the door is the special place of honor for guests and medicine men. Movement inside the hogan is always in a clockwise direction encircling the hearth.

four-sided leaning log hogan   *covered with thinner poles*   *with a final cover of adobe*

32

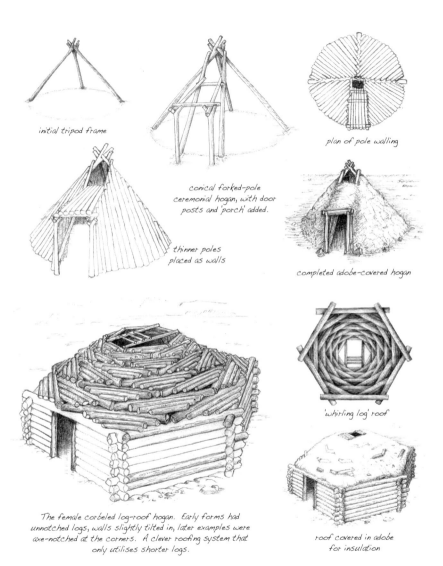

initial tripod frame

conical forked-pole
ceremonial hogan, with door
posts and 'porch' added.

thinner poles
placed as walls

plan of pole walling

completed adobe-covered hogan

The female corbeled log-roof hogan. Early forms had
unnotched logs, walls slightly tilted in, later examples were
axe-notched at the corners. A clever roofing system that
only utilises shorter logs.

'whirling log' roof

roof covered in adobe
for insulation

33

BAMBOO HUTS
watch them grow

Bamboo is an incredibly versatile building material. An entire building can be made out of it with next to no waste. It grows in hot, humid conditions across South America, Central Africa and south-east Asia, reaching heights of 75 feet and diameters of 7 inches (in exceptional cases it grows as high as 120 feet). The woody cane has exceptional strength and resilience and, being hollow, is also light and easily worked, its fine fibres giving surprising flexibility.

Bamboo is the fastest-growing plant on earth, some varieties gaining two feet per day. It reaches its full height within a year but takes 3 to 6 years to reach maximum strength. Mature straight poles are gathered in a thinning process, the plant quickly regenerating. Thicker culms are good for compression whereas the thinner ones have better elasticity and strength. As well as being quickly renewable, bamboo is cheap, easy to transport, and strong in both compression and flexion.

There are many advantages to the use of bamboo, such as simple assembly and disassembly, quick replacement and reuse of structural members and parts which can last over thirty years. Disadvantages include fast tool wear, and its tendency to rapidly rot in the ground.

Where possible, bamboo is often combined with other woods to make a more durable and taller structure, the bamboo being used for cladding or bracing, stiffening the structure in the process.

rectangular half-lap joint

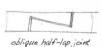
oblique half-lap joint

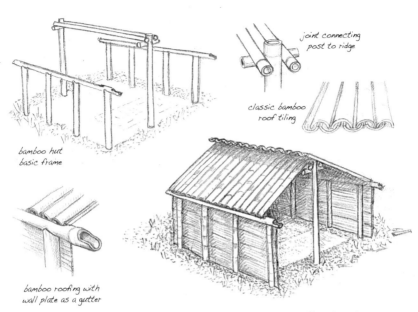

joint connecting
post to ridge

classic bamboo
roof tiling

bamboo hut
basic frame

bamboo roofing with
wall plate as a gutter

An early earth-floored bamboo hut. This is a typical bamboo design that is still used as a temporary shelter. The frame is formed by posts driven into the ground connected by a wall plate. Bamboo boards are fixed to form the walls. Self-supporting bamboo shingles are both rafters and roofing.

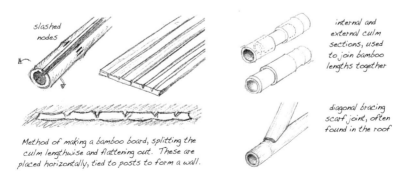

slashed
nodes

internal and
external culm
sections, used
to join bamboo
lengths together

diagonal bracing
scarf joint, often
found in the roof

Method of making a bamboo board, splitting the culm lengthwise and flattening out. These are placed horizontally, tied to posts to form a wall.

35

BAMBOO SOPHISTICATION
lashings and joints

The number of ways in which bamboo can be used is breathtaking. Canes, half-canes, laths, beading, guttering, bamboo boards, rope ties, and roof tiles are just some examples. Rope ties made from bamboo bark are saturated to make them supple, then dried into string. They are used as taut knots in lashed joints, where they sometimes pass through bored holes (*see examples below*). Bamboo joints are also shown (*opposite*).

In hot and humid bamboo–growing areas, homes need to offer protection from weather and animals while allowing excellent air ventilation. Early bamboo dwellings had earth floors, sometimes covered with mats of bamboo stems or leaves woven the same way as the walls, useful for replacing damaged wall sections at short notice. Later, floors began to be raised off the ground, using bamboo canes as floor joists and bamboo planks as floorboards (*see page 35*), creating useful space below, for storage, and often for animals. If necessary, planks can be woven to create more solid floors.

There are many options for walls. Canes can be placed in the ground to form a palisade wall linked with a rail, strips can be threaded through horizontal railings to create a vertically woven wall (*see page 55*), or poles can be laid on top of one another, horizontally held in place by two posts anchored into the ground at each corner.

 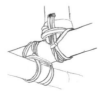 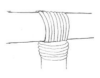

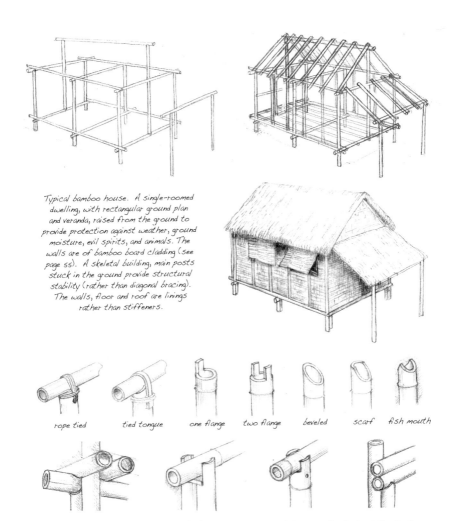

Typical bamboo house. A single-roomed dwelling, with rectangular ground plan and veranda, raised from the ground to provide protection against weather, ground moisture, evil spirits, and animals. The walls are of bamboo board cladding (see page 55). A skeletal building, main posts stuck in the ground provide structural stability (rather than diagonal bracing). The walls, floor and roof are linings rather than stiffeners.

| rope tied | tied tongue | one flange | two flange | beveled | scarf | fish mouth |

Some of the common types of bamboo joints with main joints connecting horizontal/vertical members and double beams. Facing page: Common lashed joints.

ROUNDED TIMBER-FRAMED
from circles to rectangles

Whenever available, wood has long been the material of choice for shelters the world over, being easy to shape, strong in tension and able to bend without breaking. In early stone axe cultures, saplings were the easiest to cut and were widely employed (*see 'Benders', pages 10–15*). The use of flint and later bronze brought larger poles into play, up to 6 inches wide, big enough to give rigidity in a single pole, and leading to permanent buildings with better winter insulation. Strong upright poles supported high roof rafters often with square cross-beams.

Despite these changes, however, shelters remained largely circular with climatically-influenced differences. Earth lodges and pit houses, for example (*see pages 28–29*) became prominent as stronger roof poles could support earth and sod. Japanese builders made a rough wood cone and added a sheltering cap over the smoke vent due to heavy rain.

Circular shelters are hard to expand as they rely on the length of the rafters. Around 2,500 BC the first rectangular shelters began to appear. Developing in stages over centuries from simple A-frame dwellings to systems including supports for purlins (*opposite top*), they culminate in structures such as the 100 AD farm storehouse (*opposite bottom right*). The bay system allows structures to be repeated and extended for additional storage capacity. Other structures combine similar frames with earlier technology, for example the lattice roof (*centre opposite*).

These buildings, however, rely on lashings which decay quickly. The development of jointed frames solved this problem.

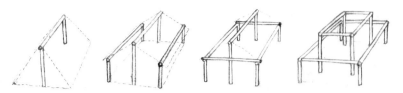

The evolution of structure, from basic A-frame to early support structures.

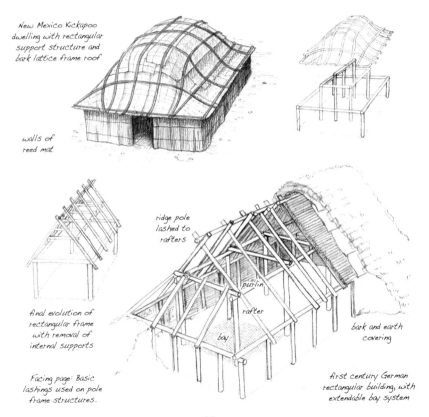

New Mexico Kickapoo dwelling with rectangular support structure and bark lattice frame roof

walls of reed mat

final evolution of rectangular frame with removal of internal supports

Facing page: Basic lashings used on pole frame structures.

ridge pole lashed to rafters

purlin

rafter

bay

bark and earth covering

first century German rectangular building, with extendable bay system

SQUARED TIMBER-FRAMED
dovetails and scarfs

Squared-sectioned timber-framed buildings represent the final evolution of crafted wooden structures. Freestanding prefabricated structures, they are jointed and pegged together, with oak being the preferred wood. Making the building off site, the carpenter treats the building as a series of frames, cross-frame, wall, floor, and roof, meticulously marking each component to ensure smooth and accurate assembly on site.

Western examples are categorized by three types of cross-frame. Firstly, post and truss, where vertical wall posts support a triangular truss (*with varying internal structural arrangements, shown opposite*). Secondly cruck frame, formed from two naturally curved timbers, connected by a tie beam, and thirdly the wide-aisled cross-frame, which again uses the basic post and truss with a lean-to added on each side so the wall posts become internal arcade posts. The cross-frames are linked lengthwise by sills, wallplates, purlins and a ridgepole, triangular bracing being added for stability. The walls are then filled with rectangular framing.

To form the walls, sections are infilled, commonly with wattle and daub, leaving the timbers exposed. Oak staves are slotted vertically 12–18in apart, and woven basket-style with hazel or cleft oak wattles later daubed on both sides with a mixture of semi-dry clay, dung and straw, finally being limewashed or painted. More narrow sections are filled with horizontal oak laths or stone slabs, then plastered with clay.

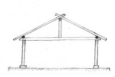  

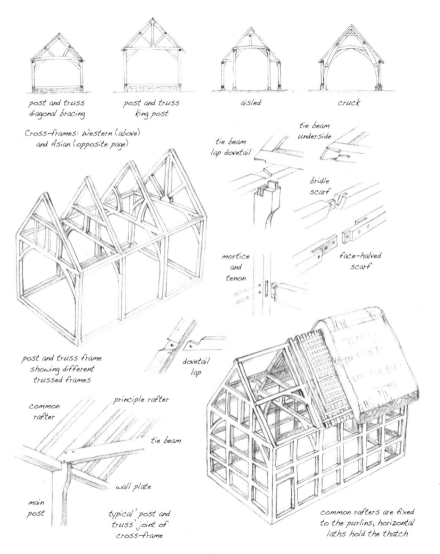

post and truss
diagonal bracing

post and truss
king post

aisled

cruck

Cross-frames: Western (above)
and Asian (opposite page)

tie beam
lap dovetail

tie beam
underside

bridle
scarf

mortice
and
tenon

face-halved
scarf

post and truss frame
showing different
trussed frames

dovetail
lap

common
rafter

principle rafter

tie beam

wall plate

main
post

typical post and
truss joint of
cross-frame

common rafters are fixed
to the purlins, horizontal
laths hold the thatch

ADOBE MUD BRICK
glorious mud

Earth is perhaps the most abundant building material available to man and its use in building goes back to the earliest times. Adobe is a soil composition of sand, clay and water with some other binding materials thrown in, often straw and dung. Wet adobe is shaped by hand or in rectangular open-framed moulds to produce bricks, approximately 14 x 16 x 12 inches, which are dried slowly in the shade to reduce the likelihood of cracking (*below*). These are used to build the walls with the sand and clay mix as the mortar. Dry dung repels insects, and straw will help the brick dry evenly.

Adobe brick houses have been commonplace for thousands of years in the Middle East, North Africa, Spain and southern North America. The hot arid climates of these regions produce few other building materials and the low rainfall also means that earth houses can survive well. These are durable, inexpensive, and simple shelters.

Adobe buildings have a low structural strength and walls tend be thick and low, with short roof spans and are often round or curved, making them slightly more stable. On hot days, thick walls warm up slowly, keeping the inside cool, while on cold nights they radiate stored heat. To prevent rain damage, walls are often given a finish of mud plaster or stucco, although some ancient cultures use lime-based cement.

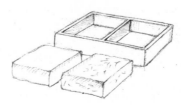

A Spanish-style adobe building, slightly less structurally stable than the example below due to its rectangular shape. The typical features of an adobe mud dwelling are apparent: protruding roof beams, thick walls with wooden lintels above the door and windows, single-storied because of its low structural strength. The typical roof construction is shown to the right.

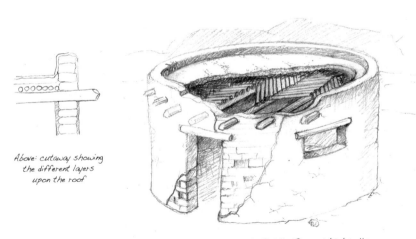

Above: cutaway showing the different layers upon the roof

Above: A New Mexico round adobe dwelling, 16 ft in diameter and 8 ft tall. The mud brick walls are covered with adobe plaster on both exterior and interior walls. Protruding roof beams or 'viga' are laid across the wall, while smaller poles between them serve as rafters in a zigzag formation. The roof is then covered with 8 inches of insulating earth.

STRAW BALES
from harvest to home

Straw bale buildings first appeared in the late 1800s in the Nebraska Sandhills, USA, where settlers discovered a climate of baking hot summers and bitterly wind-chilled winters, a terrain without trees or stones, and a soil too sandy for sod construction. What they did have, however, were acres of land suitable for grain crops, a harvest by-product of woody straw stems, and newly invented baling machines.

Bales provide excellent heat and sound insulation, and are strong in compression. Their use today is under continual development and refinement, with interest spreading worldwide.

A straw bale house is based upon a stone foundation with a slate damp course. It must be a draining foundation, at least 9 inches high to avoid rain splash back. Upon this the walls are designed in bale lengths, with openings for windows which have to be at least one bale length from the corner and should not exceed 50% of the wall area. A load bearing frame is placed within windows and doors with a settlement gap left above each one. Above this, the roof must overhang the walls by at least 18 inches at the eaves. Also vital is a robust and wall-width wallplate to distribute the roof load equally.

Bales are staked together vertically and the walls finally plastered.

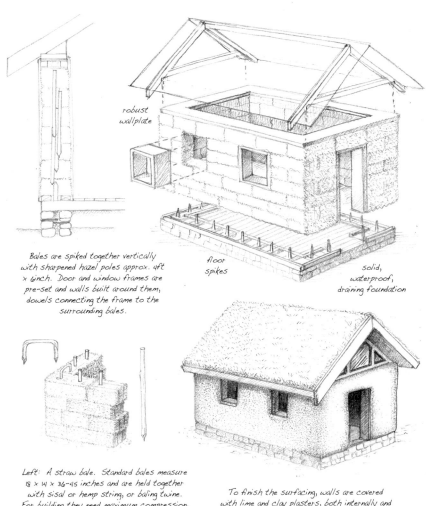

robust
wallplate

floor
spikes

solid,
waterproof,
draining foundation

Bales are spiked together vertically
with sharpened hazel poles approx. 4ft
× 6inch. Door and window frames are
pre-set and walls built around them,
dowels connecting the frame to the
surrounding bales.

Left: A straw bale. Standard bales measure
18 × 14 × 36-45 inches and are held together
with sisal or hemp string, or baling twine.
For building they need maximum compression,
about a third more straw than usual. They
have to be kept dry during construction.

To finish the surfacing, walls are covered
with lime and clay plasters, both internally and
externally. After this has dried they can be
painted with limewash or porous paints.

45

IGLOOS
it's cold outside

The Igloo or 'snow house' was developed for the tundras of the arctic, and is used as a winter home or temporary base for a hunting party. Although usually 6–15 ft in diameter (depending on the intended length of use), some communal igloos are as big as 20 ft.

Igloos are best built on a slope, so the cold air drops to the tools and storage areas, leaving the bed area warmed by blubber lamps. Building takes two men only a few hours. Snow blocks, 3 ft long, 1½ ft wide and 8 inches high, are excavated from the intended floor after checking for correct snow consistency. The first layer is set into a circle and then trimmed at an angle so that the dome's blocks spiral upwards. Blocks are cut large, trimmed into place and finally banged together, causing ice crystals to melt and refreeze, so welding them into place.

Igloos, like all spheres, offer maximum volume with minimum surface area and have no corners for cold air to gather. A lining of caribou hide is often added for further insulation, which also traps a layer of cold air between the skin and the wall, preventing melting.

Igloos can be extended by covered passageways linking to other domes, an important consideration within highly social communities forced by extreme weather to spend long periods indoors. They are left standing for the use of any traveller that passes along the same route.

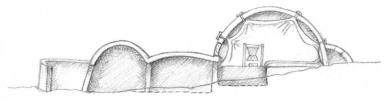

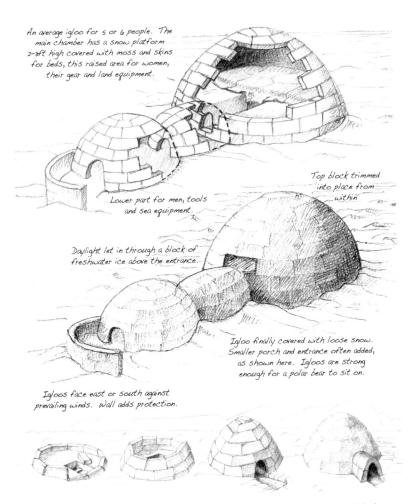

An average igloo for 5 or 6 people. The main chamber has a snow platform 2-3ft high covered with moss and skins for beds, this raised area for women, their gear and land equipment.

Top block trimmed into place from within

Lower part for men, tools and sea equipment.

Daylight let in through a block of freshwater ice above the entrance.

Igloo finally covered with loose snow. Smaller porch and entrance often added, as shown here. Igloos are strong enough for a polar bear to sit on.

Igloos face east or south against prevailing winds. Wall adds protection.

Construction of an igloo, showing initial spiral and tunnel excavated lower than internal level so that cold air remains in lower porch area, trapped by a skin door.

47

GEODESIC DOMES
new uses for ancient geometry

The term geodesic dome was coined by the inventor Buckminster Fuller, who popularized them as an alternative housing solution in the 1950s and 60s. However, the first recorded example was built in 1922 in Jena, Germany, under the guidance of Dr Walter Bauersfield, to house a planetarium. Geodesy is the science of measuring the size and shape of the Earth, and a geodesic is the shortest distance between two points on its surface.

Geodesic domes have been included in this book because of their appealing aesthetics and relative simplicity of construction. They come in a bewildering variety of shapes and sizes, and can be constructed in a number of different ways. The icosahedron-based examples shown opposite and on the next page are pole-based domes, which can be made from bamboo, broomstick handles, or lengths of metal tubing.

The key to successful dome building and assembly lies in the junctions. Two possibilities are illustrated below, a third is to fit hosepipe to the ends, flatten, drill and bolt through. Plates can also be useful, or if using metal tubing the tips can be hammered flat and a single hole drilled through for a bolt and wing nut.

worzel joint   *drainage pipe joint*

ICOSAHEDRON

Note the shaded triangular face. It will be subdivided in the examples which follow

A pentagonal tent based on the icosahedron.

Note that any polygonal base can make a tent in much the same way.

2-FREQUENCY ICOSAHEDRON

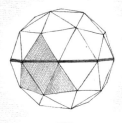

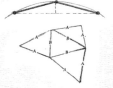

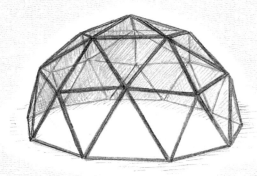

The basic 2-frequency icosahedral dome. Two strut lengths are required: A: 30 poles × 0.273 and B: 35 poles × 0.309 of the diameter (see appendix). The equator of the sphere forms the base-line. The dome can be raised by adding a drum or cylinder below the equator (e.g. shown centre opposite).

49

More Complex Domes
subdividing the triangles

There are five ways to subdivide the surface of a sphere so that each resulting face is an identical regular polygon. These are known as the five Platonic solids or regular polyhedra: the tetrahedron, octahedron, cube, icosahedron and dodecahedron (*shown left to right below*). The geodesic domes shown over these two pages are derived from the icosahedron, often the best candidate, but domes can also be constructed from the other Platonic, and even Archimedean solids, and some examples from octahedra and even cuboctahedra are shown in the appendix (*pages 56–58*). Note that some domes possess a natural equator, whereas others (eg the 3-frequency icosahedral dome (*opposite top*) use a cutoff line above or below the equator.

Domes can be covered in canvas, plastic, bark, skins, old parachutes or any locally available material, with the covering either on top of the frame, or suspended inside it (often preferable for larger structures). A large dome can pack into a surprisingly small space. In more permanent versions triangular panels can be cut for the faces from wood, plastic, or glass to allow the light in.

Icosahedral geodesic domes, with their pentagonal geometry are one of the best ways to get to know the special golden section symmetry which defines most biological life on earth.

3-FREQUENCY ICOSAHEDRON

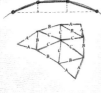

A 3-frequency icosahedral dome. Three strut lengths are required to make this, A: 30 poles × 0.1743, B: 55 poles × 0.2018 and C: 80 poles × 0.2062 of the diameter. Please see the appendix on pages 56-58 for the mapping diagram. Note that this dome is slightly more than a hemisphere as, like all odd-number frequency icosahedral domes, it does not possess a true equator.

4-FREQUENCY ICOSAHEDRON

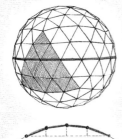

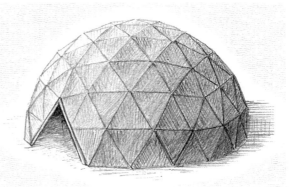

A 4-frequency icosahedral dome. Six strut lengths are needed: A: 30 × 0.1266, B: 60 × 0.1473, C: 30 × 0.1476, D: 30 × 0.1493, E: 70 × 0.1564 and F: 30 × 0.1625 of the intended diameter. Doors and porches can be fitted in any number of imaginative ways to geodesic domes. Domes can also be joined together in giant bubble-like structures.

ORIENTATION AND SYMBOLISM
images of higher realities

Many peoples worldwide see their traditional dwellings as scaled down versions of a hierarchical universe, and portray their cosmological scheme in the layout, orientation and decoration of everything around them. In the Mongolian Ger the roof represents the sky and heavenly vault, the crown is the sun and entrance to the upper world, and the two roof poles (*bagana*) are the world tree leading to the upper world. In the *nuhwe* or meeting house of the Colombian Kogi tribe, everything descends from the central cross-beams on which the universe is built, their nine worlds are represented in rings in the roof, and hammocks suspend sleepers between the different worlds. The perimeter of an ancient dwelling encloses a sacred space, the doorway threshold being the sacred transitional gateway between the outer and inner realms.

The circle (or sphere) is the traditional symbol of unity and the infinite, the ceiling of dwellings generally representing the heavens, dome of the sky. The universally traditional square-in-circle symbolism of union between heaven and earth can also be found in dwellings across the world. In pit houses (*below*) and earth lodges, the impression gazing upwards is of a squared roof poles formation, an ever-present reaffirmation of the four cardinal directions.

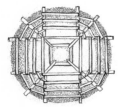
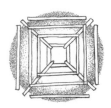

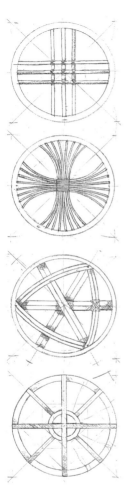

stripes:
rainbow

curved
mounds:
prayer
places

white disks:
stars and
constellations

dotted stripe:
trail of spirit
animal

stars
on earth

Above: Tipi symbolism of the Blackfeet tribe. The dark top and bottom backgrounds represent earth and sky respectively. The light background is for the vision painting, usually an animal figure.

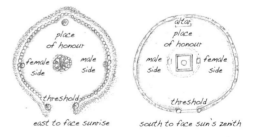

place
of honour

female
side

male
side

threshold

east to face sunrise

altar,
place
of honour

male
side

female
side

threshold

south to face sun's zenith

Looking up: Designs of four different yurt-type crowns, based on either a four or six.

Plan of the forked-pole hogan (left) and the yurt (right). Movement in both occurs in the 'sunwise' direction and both are genderly segregated with a hearth at the centre.

CLADDING AND FINISHING
covering and ornament

Cladding is the final stage of work in the construction of most simple shelters, providing its enveloping skin. It generally offers minimal structural support although it sometimes has bracing properties. At its most basic cladding provides privacy and defines a boundary, but it can also provide thermal insulation, weatherproofing and defence against foes, little and large. As with everything we have seen in this book cladding materials depend on a combination of local availability and climatic conditions. So, cladding in hot areas allows air ventilation whereas in cold and wet areas cladding invariably protects against snow and ice and also provides insulation. Common cladding materials include leaves, animal skins, bark, felt, woven bamboo panels, reed mattings, earth. Examples are shown opposite.

This book has hopefully reminded many readers of the immense variety of inspirational indigenous dwellings from around the world, to sit alongside the better-known forms of tipi and yurt. Like our fellow animals, humans build nests too, and adapting oneself to the environment rather than adapting the environment to oneself (to suit purely human needs) is a helpful position to maintain in order to stay integral to and respectful of nature. Traditional societies achieve this by viewing themselves within an all embracing cosmological framework where all parts are interdependent, in order to sustain a balanced and harmonious existence. It is not hard to do if you try.

So, for those with a creative eye and a practical mind, there should be enough in these pages to build, experience, and marvel at these beautiful and ingenious structures, and spend more time in the heart of nature.

bamboo vertical poles, common wall infill on Asian dwellings

bamboo board used on bamboo huts and other Asian shelters

decorative herring-bone bamboo board

trellis and felt covering widely used in yurts

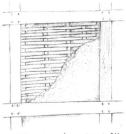

wattle and daub, used as infill in timber-frame buildings

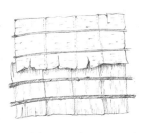

birch bark secured by string, over elm bark secured by saplings, on benders

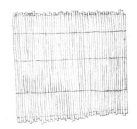

reed matting used on benders and round pole shelters

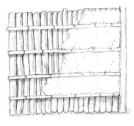

vertical poles with mud plaster, used on African conical huts

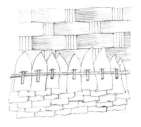

bamboo leaf cladding used on African woven shelters

APPENDIX -- SELECTED DOMES

CENTRED CUBOCTAHEDRAL DOME

A = 0.38269 x 16
B = 0.5 x 12

NOTE: ALL STRUT LENGTHS FOR DOME DIAMETER 1

Note: All lengths are sections of great circles, so the dome can be made of just 6 long bendy poles overhead plus two for the base.

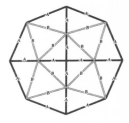

2-FREQUENCY CUBOCTAHEDRAL DOME

A = 0.19509 x 24
B = 0.21146 x 24
C = 0.25882 x 30
D = 0.2706 x 12
E = 0.28868 x 12

Note: This dome is also adaptable to long section poles and has a a a triangle overhead which can be left open for a smoke opening.

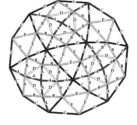

3-FREQUENCY CUBOCTAHEDRAL DOME

A = 0.1274 x 24
B = 0.13677 x 12
C = 0.13734 x 24
D = 0.137845 x 24
E = 0.14541 x 24
F = 0.165965 x 30
G = 0.178705 x 30
H = 0.18173 x 24
I = 0.18898 x 27
J = 0.192585 x 24

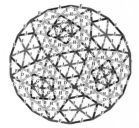

3-FREQUENCY OCTAHEDRAL DOME

A = 0.19509 x 32
B = 0.21146 x 24
C = 0.25882 x 24
D = 0.2706 x 12
E = 0.28868 x 12

Note: A good design for a medium-sized dome requiring orientation to the four directions.

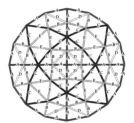

56

2-FREQUENCY ICOSAHEDRAL DOME

A = 0.273265 x 30
B = 0.309015 x 35

NOTE: ALL STRUT
LENGTHS FOR
DOME DIAMETER 1

Note: One of the most simple and satisfying 5-symmetry domes to construct. Just two strut lengths.

GREAT CIRCLE ICOSIDODECAHEDRAL DOME

A = 0.18142 x 32
B = 0.27327 x 32
C = 0.32043 x 32

Note: This dome of half great circles can be made from just 14 long bendy poles plus two for the base. Just add together the lengths and mark the junction points.

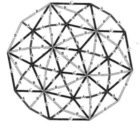

3-FREQUENCY ICOSAHEDRAL DOME

A = 0.17431 x 30
B = 0.201775 x 55
C = 0.206205 x 80

Note: An excellent choice for a larger dome. Only three strut lengths.

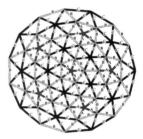

4-FREQUENCY ICOSAHEDRAL DOME

A = 0.12659 x 30
B = 0.147265 x 60
C = 0.14762 x 30
D = 0.149295 x 30
E = 0.156435 x 70
F = 0.16246 x 30

Note: Suitable for really big domes. Some elements can be stored intact and folded, e.g., the 5A stars and 4E2D stars.

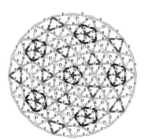

APPENDIX - SELECTED DOMES

5-FREQUENCY
ICOSAHEDRAL DOME

A = 0.099075 x 30
B = 0.112845 x 60
C = 0.1158 x 30
D = 0.115895 x 30
E = 0.122545 x 80
F = 0.122675 x 20
G = 0.12362 x 70
H = 0.127585 x 70
I = 0.1308 x 35

Note: As domes
increase in
complexity and
size it is vital to
make strut lengths
as accurately as
possible.

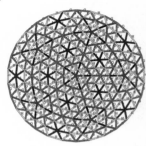

6-FREQUENCY
ICOSAHEDRAL DOME

A = 0.081285 x 30
B = 0.090955 x 60
C = 0.09369 x 30
D = 0.09524 x 30
E = 0.099005 x 60
F = 0.10141 x 90
G = 0.102955 x 130
H = 0.107675 x 65
I = 0.108315 x 60

Note: All
even-numbered
frequency domes
have a genuine
equator.

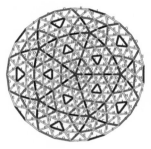

7-FREQUENCY
ICOSAHEDRAL DOME

A = 0.06887 x 30
B = 0.075985 x 60
C = 0.07832 x 30
D = 0.08077 x 30
E = 0.0824 x 60
F = 0.08533 x 30
G = 0.08549 x 60
H = 0.08566 x 60

I = 0.086765 x 80
J = 0.087925 x 90
K = 0.090775 x 70
L = 0.090805 x 35
M = 0.091185 x 70
N = 0.09274 x 70
O = 0.093955 x 30

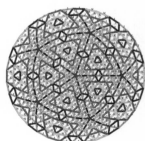

BUCKMINSTER FULLER'S BAMBOO CROSS DOME

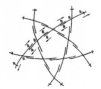